1

LETTERS & ALPHABETS

LETTRES & ALPHABETS

LETTERN & ALPHABETE

LETTERE ed ALFABETI

LETRAS & ALFABETOS

文字 & アルファベット

字母時空

LETTERS & ALPHABETS

DOVERPICTURA

DOVER PUBLICATIONS, Inc. | Mineola, New York

Selected and designed by Thalia Large and Alan Weller.

Letters & Alphabets is a new work, first published by Dover Publications, Inc., in 2004.

The CD-ROM file names correspond to the images in the book. All of the artwork
stored on the CD-ROM can be imported directly into a wide range of design and
word-processing programs on either Windows or Macintosh platforms. No further
installation is necessary.

International Standard Book Number: 0-486-99635-2

Manufactured in Hong Kong
Dover Publications, Inc., 31 East 2nd Street, Mineola, NY 11501
www.doverpublications.com

3

4

5

6

7

8

9

10

11

12

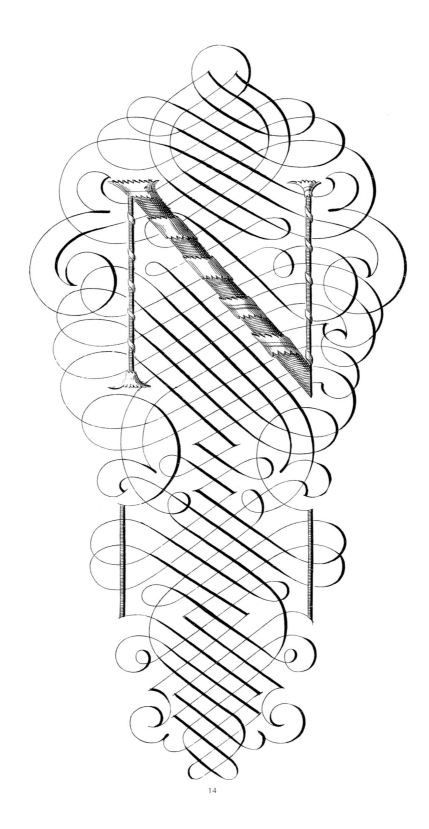

14

15

16

17

19

20

21

22

23

24

25

26

27

28–30   31–33   34–36

37

38

39

40

41

42

43

44

45

46

47

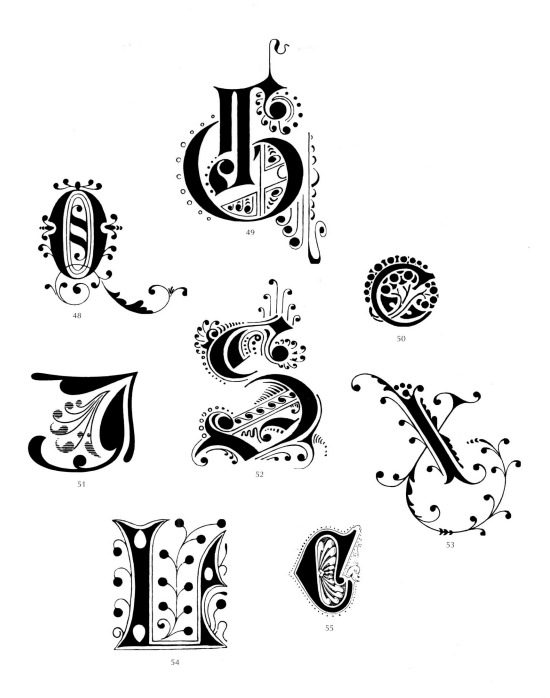

48

49

50

51

52

53

54

55

56

57

58

59

60

61

62

63

64

65

66

67

68

69

70

71

72–74

75–77

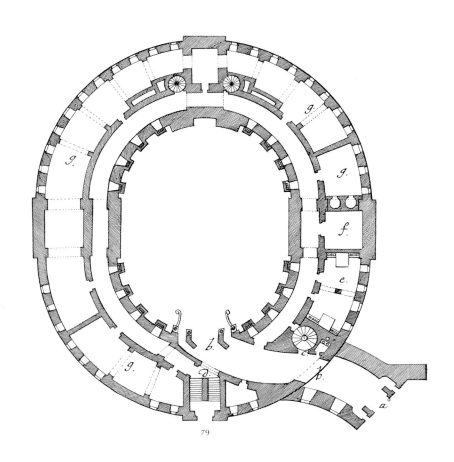

79

32

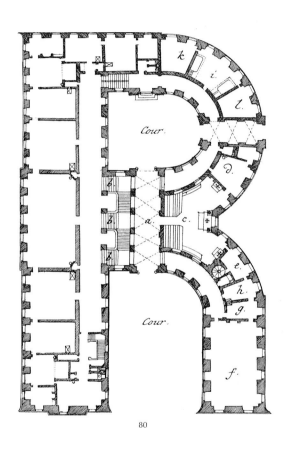

80

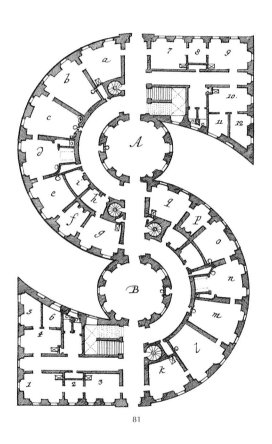

81

83

84

85

86

87

88

89

90

91

92

93

94

95

96

97

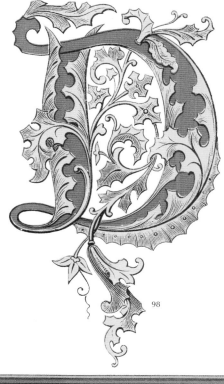

98

99

100

101

39

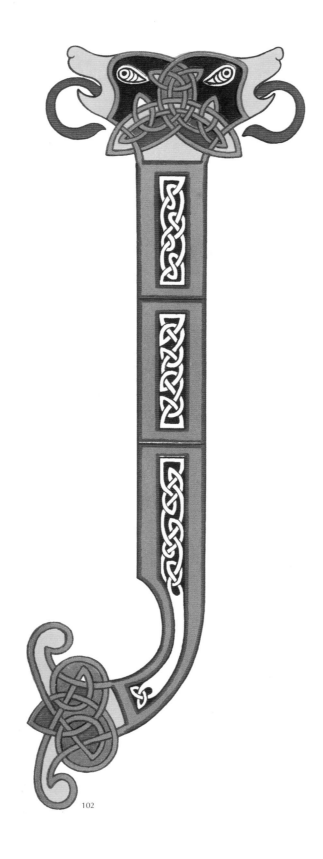

102

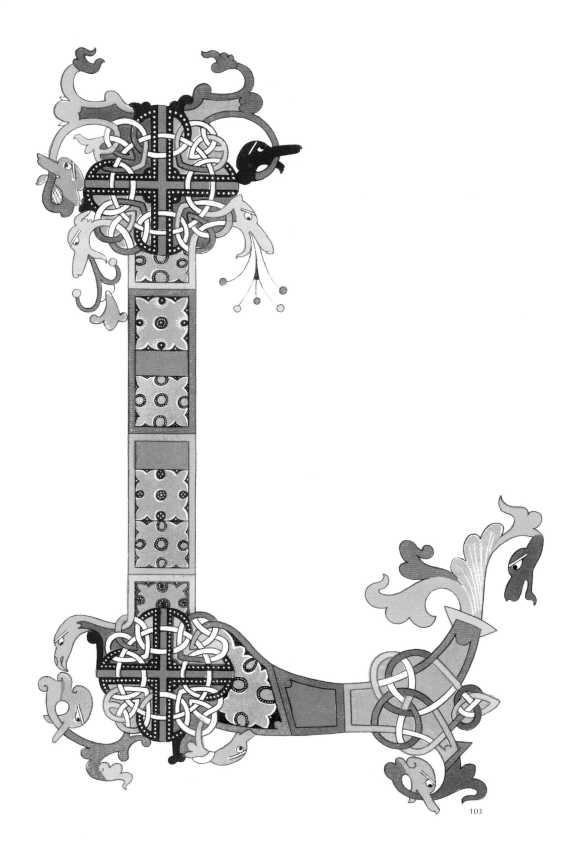

103

104

105

106

107

108

109

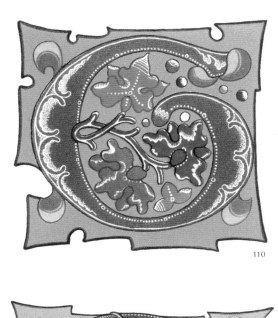

110

111

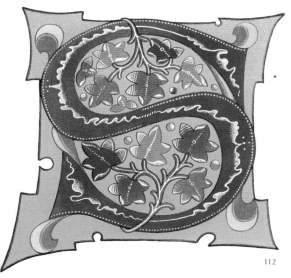

112

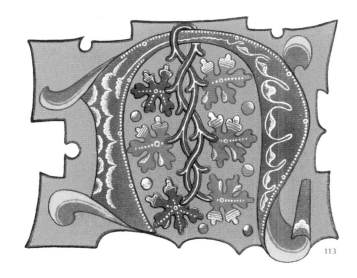

113

114

115, 116

117, 118

119

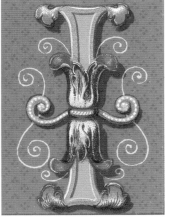

120–123

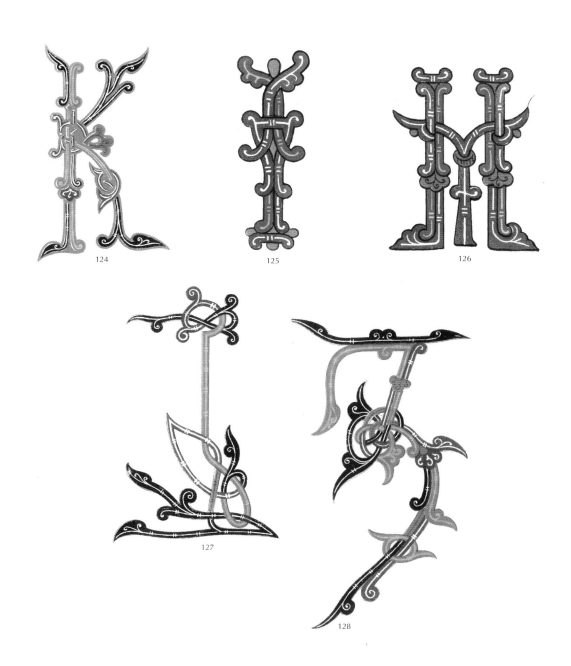

124

125

126

127

128

129–132

133–136

137

138

139

140

141

142

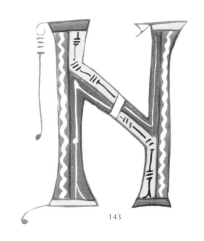

143

144

145

146

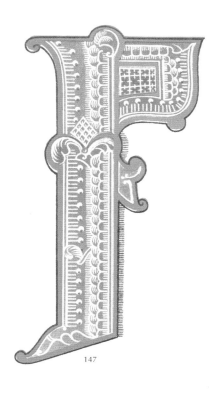

147

148

149

150

151

152

153

154

155

156

157

158

159

160

161

162

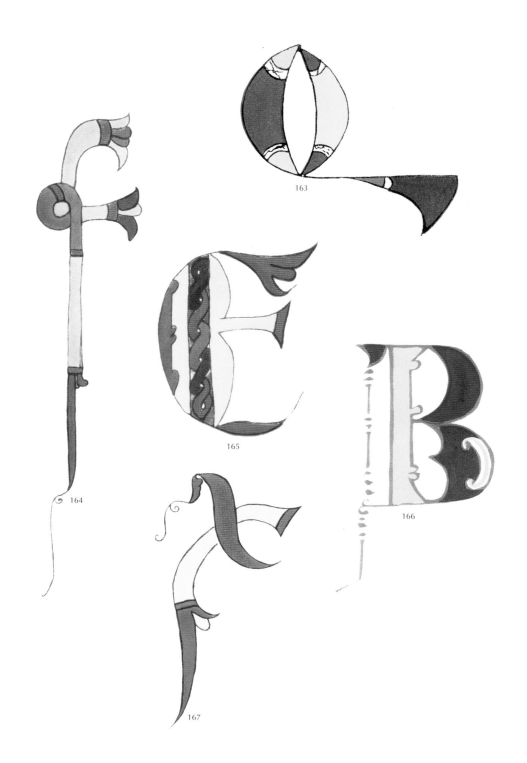

163

164

165

166

167

168–170

171–173

174–176

177–179

180–182

183–185

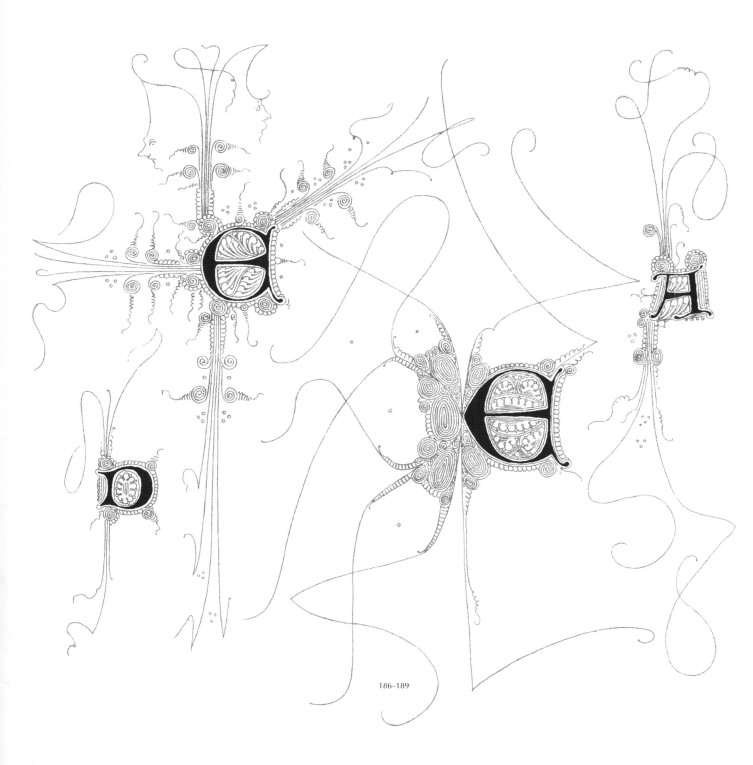

186–189

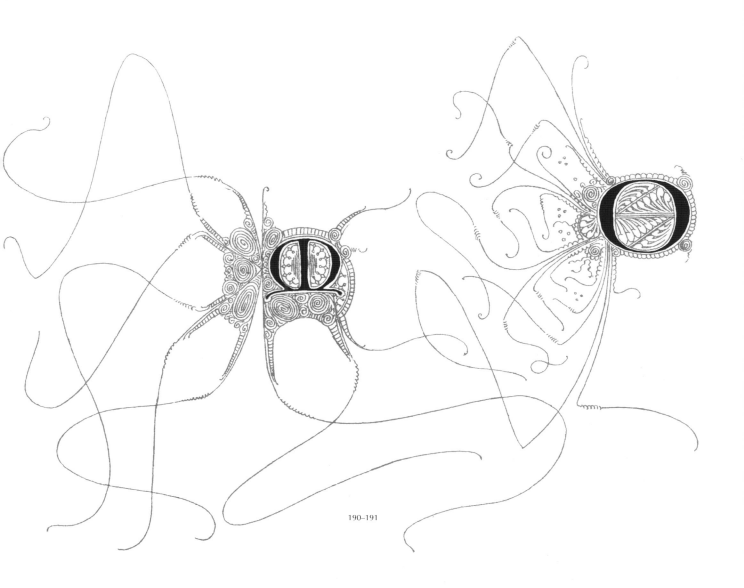

190–191

192

193

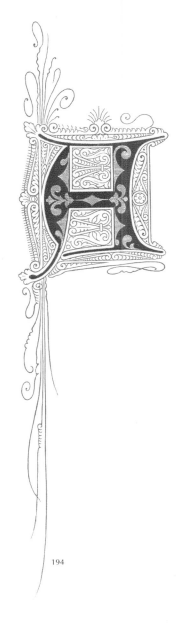

194

195

196

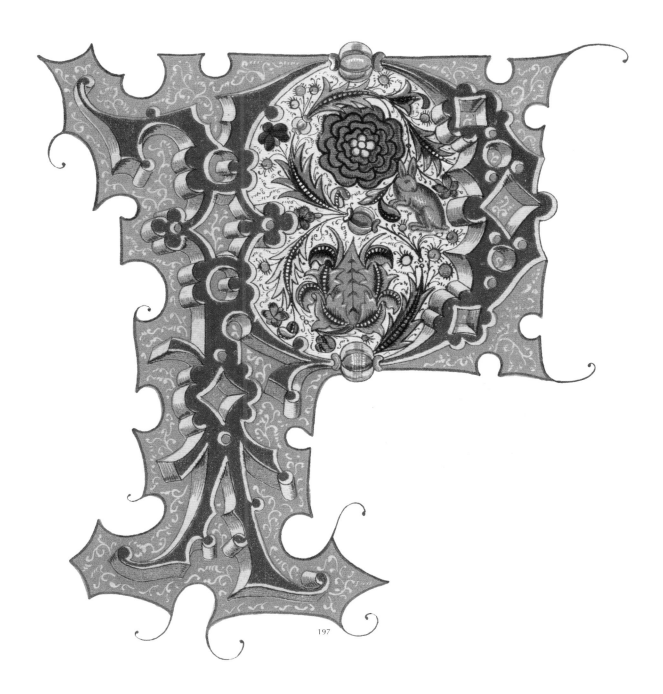

197

198

199

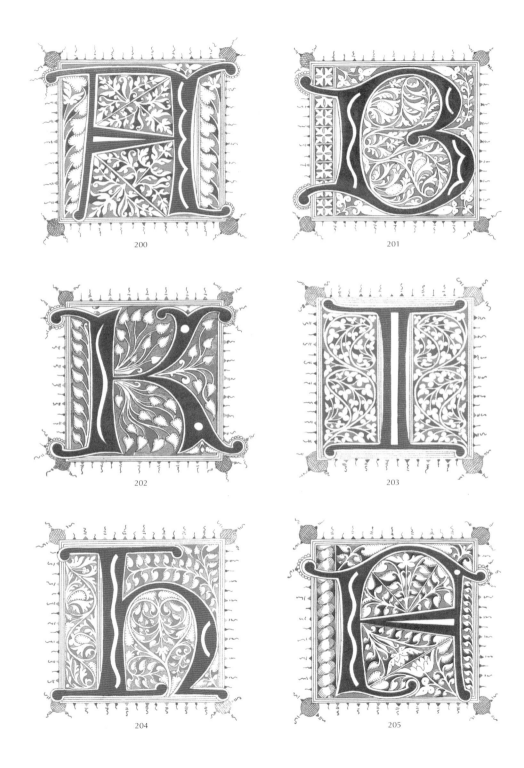

200

201

202

203

204

205

206

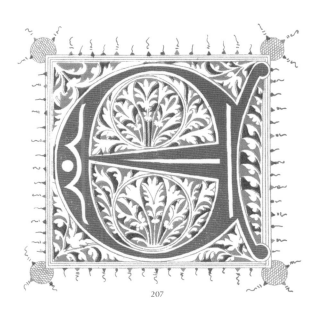

207

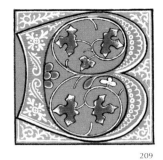

208

209

210

214

215

216

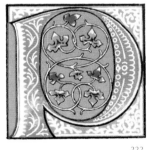

220

221

222

226

227

228

211

212

213

217

218

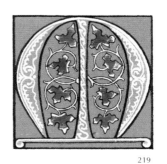

219

223

224

225

229

230`

231

232

233

234

235

236

237

238

239

240

241

242

243

244

245

246

247

248

249

250

251

252

253

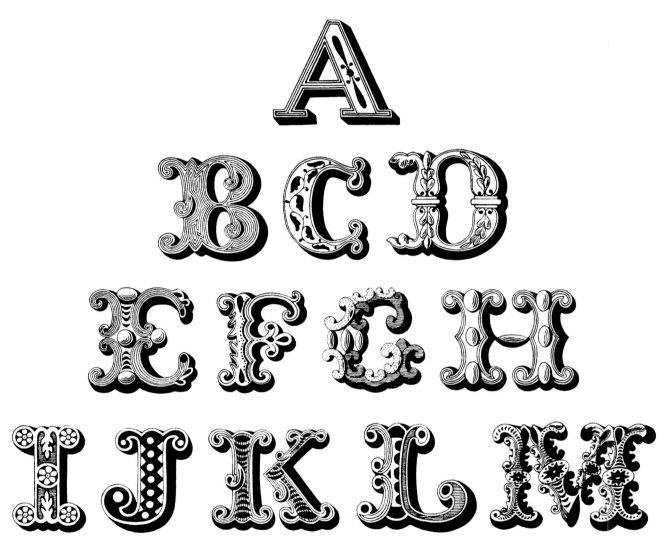

254–266

N O P Q R
S T U V
W X Y
Z

267–279

280

281

282

283

284

285

286

287   288   289   290

291   292   293

294   295   296

297   298   299

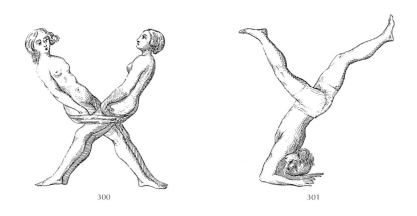

300

301

302

303–305

310–312

316–318

322–324

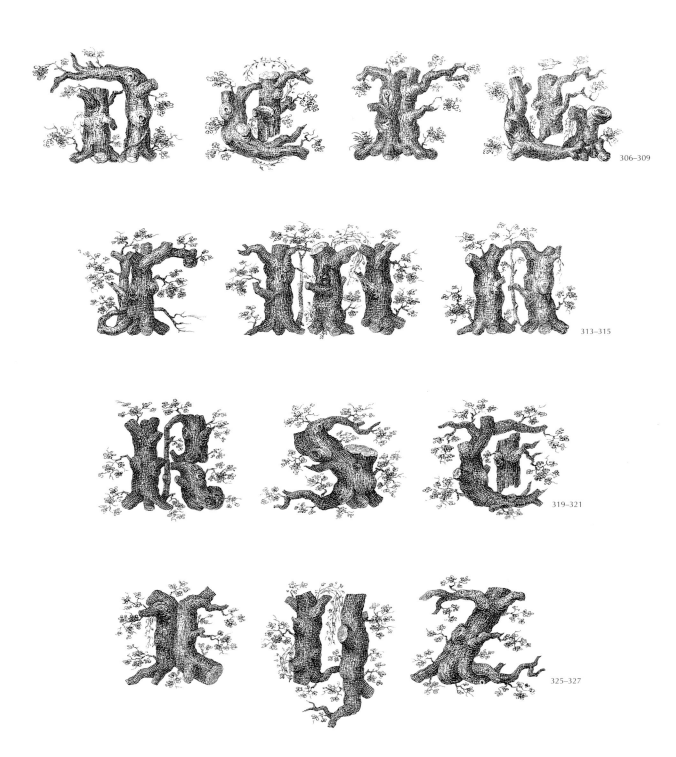

306–309

313–315

319–321

325–327

328–330

331–333

334–336

337–339

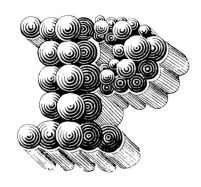 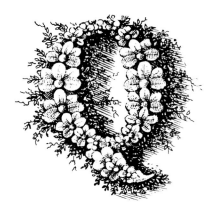 

346, 347

348–350

351, 352

353

354

355

356

357

358

359

360

361

362

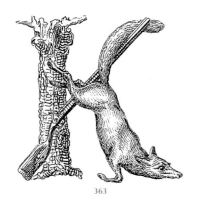

363

364

365

366 367 368

369 370 371

372 373 374

375

376

377

378

379

380

381

382

383

384

385

386

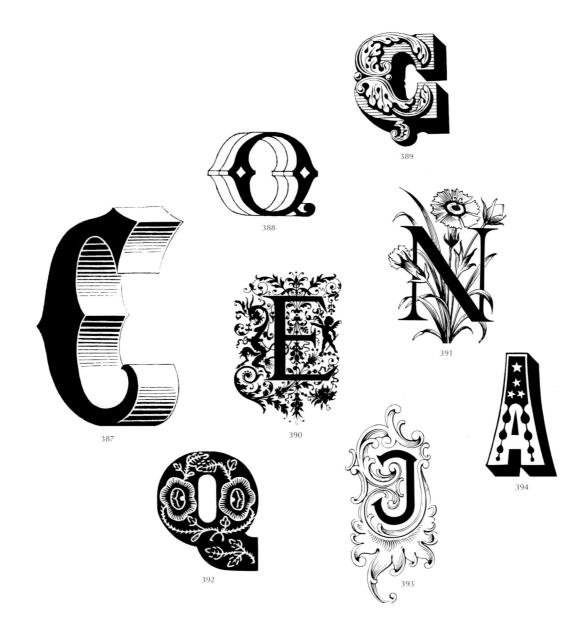

389

388

387

390

391

392

393

394

395

396

397

398

399

400

401

402

403

404

405

406

407

408

409

410

411

412

413

414

415

416

417

418–422

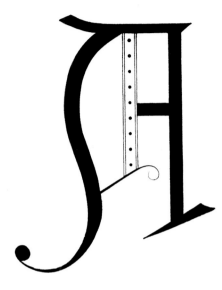

423–430

431–438

103

439–446

447–454

455–461

462–469

470–478

479–486

487–495

496–503

111

504–512

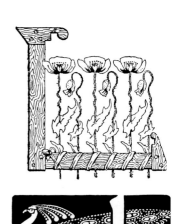

513–522

537–544

545–552

553–560

561–568

569–576

577–586

121

587–595

596–603

604–611

612–619

620–627

628–634